To my family and those I call family -
thank you for all your love and constant
encouragement. The world is more
beautiful because of you.

The Lone Princess

Copyright © 2021 by Marlea Louviere

ISBN: 978-0-578-25790-7

Written and Illustrated by Marlea Louviere

Edited by Daphne Kirk and Michele Louviere

Graphic Edit by Hannah Heneghan

Gallia - God shall redeem

Elora - God is light

There once was a young princess named Gallia, who lived in a giant castle. For many years, Princess Gallia lived alone, far from her father, the King, and all those she called friend.

In her castle were many rooms - so many that Princess Gallia found it easy to get lost in her giant castle.

But Princess Gallia only liked going to certain rooms. She did not feel comfortable going to the rooms that made her feel scared. She preferred not to remember or think about those rooms. So she locked those doors, just in case she accidentally tried to open one of them.

Thankfully, Princess Gallia had a few favorite rooms. She loved going into her playroom, which was overflowing with wonderful books, crafts, and toys. Princess Gallia often pretended she was far, far away on a beautiful adventure. She often created stories of a different life than the one inside her castle.

She also loved going to the kitchen in her castle. The kitchen smelled scrumptious and was overflowing with tasty food, so she went there often. Princess Gallia didn't like feeling empty, and the kitchen was full of delicious food that made her feel whole.

Princess Gallia often went to her sparkly bathroom. It had a big tub, and she liked filling it with warm water, bubbles, and toys.

She took lots of baths because she often felt dirty inside.
Baths made her feel clean, at least for a while.

Sometimes, Princess Gallia would climb, climb, climb her tower where the big window was. She would look outside and watch other children and families playing together.

One day, while sitting in her tower, she noticed a lady, carrying a basket, walking towards her giant castle. No one had come to visit her in a very long time - the princess was just simply too busy in her castle to have time for family or friends.

Princess Gallia ran to her big door and looked out the
little window to see who it was. She recognized the lady
as someone known to be a safe, caring, and honoring
helper. Many days, Princess Gallia had seen this kind lady
care for childen near her castle walls. After some thought,
Princess Gallia decided she felt safe to invite her in for a visit.

Princess Gallia opened the door, and the Lady smiled at her. She leaned down to show Princess Gallia that she had bought cookies and muffins in her basket and introduced herself saying, "Hi, my name is Lady Elora."

She gave Princess Gallia the basket and asked if she could come back tomorrow with more. Princess Gallia thought for a moment. With a nod and a shy smile, she said, "Yes, I'd like that."

For many weeks, Princess Gallia's new friend came with a basket every day. And every time she came, Princess Gallia let her come further into her giant castle. She showed her all her favorite rooms, the playroom, the kitchen, the bathroom, and the tower room.

One day, Lady Elora asked her where she slept at night. After all, the princess had shown her many rooms in her giant castle, but not her bedroom.

Princess Gallia's bedroom wasn't a room she liked, and it was far away from her favorite rooms. Her bedroom held the castle's lone mirror. For many reasons, ones she avoided thinking of, she didn't like going into her bedroom.

"I'll go with you inside, and I'll stay with you. When you want to leave, we can leave," Lady Elora gently offered.

Princess Gallia sighed and thought about going into this room with Lady Elora. Finally, with a nod and bowed head, she softly said, "Okay."

Princess Gallia and Lady Elora journeyed to her bedroom. When they finally got to her room, Princess Gallia decided to open the door herself. She took out a key she used to lock the doors in her castle and slowly opened the door.

Her bedroom held many items, including boxes she had taped shut and stored away. The boxes were stacked tall and blocked her bed, furniture, and the lone castle mirror lying in the corner. Lady Elora gently offered to sort through the boxes with her.

Princess Gallia decided she needed to see what was in the boxes, even though the thought of opening the boxes scared and overwhelmed her. The princess realized how tired and weary she was and that if she wanted to rest, she needed to find a place for all the things in her room.

For many, many days, Princess Gallia's friend came to the castle. They went up, up, up to her room and curiously explored through the boxes. Sometimes Princess Gallia felt gross and shameful going through the boxes and would run to her sparkly bathroom for a bath.

Sometimes she felt so very sad and would run to her playroom and daydream of adventures elsewhere. And other times, Princess Gallia felt lost and incredibly lonely. Then she'd race to the kitchen so she'd be full in her belly and not empty in her heart.

Sometimes, Princess Gallia wanted to stop, but Lady Elora reminded her why they were working to find a place for everything. As she shared time and time again, the goal is not to get rid of anything or say anything wasn't important, but to put it in the right place, help her understand it, and give it meaning after being stored away for so long.

It took a very long time, and it was hard work. Sometimes the princess found more boxes in the room, making it take even longer. But, the young princess held onto hope that all of her room would be fully and truly seen.

Then; one day, Princess Gallia and her friend climbed, climbed, climbed up to her bedroom, as they have been doing. Upon entering the room, Princess Gallia realized that all the boxes had been sorted through, and she could now see her mirror.

Walking slowly holding Lady Elora's hand, she stood in front of her lone mirror. Princess Gallia's friend smiled warmly at her and said, "Now you can see what I see... that all of you is beautiful and every room in your castle is cherished because you are cherished. Princess Gallia, you are beloved to me and to the King."

And Princess Gallia cried and cried. The princess's tears helped soothe and heal the rooms that held her story. Lady Elora's presence provided the safety for Princess Gallia to grieve her once unwitnessed and hidden pain.

Turning to Lady Elora with a gentle smile, Princess Gallia said, "I have other rooms in my castle I'd like to show you." With a hopeful expression the princess added, "And I would like to show the King and others, who are as caring as you, my castle."

And she did. But not before she finally rested.

To be known and loved is the most wondrous of gifts in this world. Beloved, you are cherished and loved by your heavenly King. You are beautiful in His sight, and He knows you well.

You are altogether beautiful, my darling,
there is no flaw in you.

Song of Solomon 4:7

Thank you to all of the Lady Elora's, those called counselors, friend, those who bring the hope of healing, and those who stay in our castles holding moments of pain as well as the moments of clarity and joy.

A note to the reader:

How I wish that I could sit and talk with you as you finish reading Princess Gallia's story. I wonder if you found yourself wishing you could lock away the painful pieces of your story as easily as Princess Gallia had done. Perhaps, as you read, you realized that you too often escape in ways that only keep you safe for a moment and then end too quickly. Maybe the ways you escape add to your shame or sorrow. Or perhaps you long for someone to come to you and offer help and care as Lady Elora did for Princess Gallia. Maybe staying in your castle and not letting anyone in feels safer than allowing someone to see the rooms that hold your wounded story.

I pray that whatever your locked rooms are, you will first honor them for providing some safety. Then, I pray, that you, along with a safe helper, will work to heal and integrate your story. As you heal your story, I hope that you experience true intimacy with the King of Kings and then others in the midst of the wounds your story may hold. While these are all my longings for you, I am sure you have longings of your own. If you are interested in healing your story, wondering what 'story work' means, or finding a counselor trained to help heal stories, then go to: www.byronkehler.com

With hope for many to find healing.

Marlea Louviere

www.ingramcontent.com/pod-product-compliance
Lightning Source LLC
Chambersburg PA
CBHW041512280526
45792CB00004B/1229